SHEARSMAN
111 & 112

SPRING 2017

EDITOR
TONY FRAZER

Shearsman magazine is published in the United Kingdom by
Shearsman Books Ltd
50 Westons Hill Drive
Emersons Green
BRISTOL   BS16 7DF

Registered office: 30-31 St James Place, Mangotsfield, Bristol BS16 9JB
(this address not for correspondence)

www.shearsman.com

ISBN 978-1-84861-513-7
ISSN 0260-8049

This compilation copyright © Shearsman Books Ltd., 2017.
All rights in the works printed here revert to their authors, translators or original copyright-holders after publication. Permissions requests may be directed to *Shearsman*, but they will be forwarded to the copyright-holders.

Subscriptions and single copies

Current subscriptions—covering two double-issues, with an average length of 108 pages—cost £16 for delivery to U.K. addresses, £18 for the rest of Europe (including the Republic of Ireland), and £21 for the rest of the world. Longer subscriptions may be had for a pro-rata higher payment. North American customers will find that buying single copies from online retailers in the U.S.A. or Canada will be cheaper than subscribing. This is because airmail postage rates in the U.K. have risen rapidly, whereas copies of the magazine are printed in the U.S.A. to meet demand from online retailers there, and thus avoid the transatlantic mail and its onerous costs.

Back issues from n° 63 onwards (uniform with this issue) cost £8.95 / $16 through retail outlets. Single copies can be ordered for £8.95 direct from the press, post-free within the U.K., through the Shearsman Books online store, or from bookshops. Issues of the previous pamphlet-style version of the magazine, from n° 1 to n° 62, may be had for £3 each, direct from the press, where copies are still available, but contact us for a quote for a full, or partial, run.

Submissions

Shearsman operates a submissions-window system, whereby submissions are only accepted during the months of March and September, when selections are made for the October and April issues, respectively. Submissions may be sent by mail or email, but email attachments—other than PDFs—are not accepted. We aim to respond within 3 months of the window's closure, i.e. all who submit *should* hear by the end of June or December, although for recent issues we have often taken a month longer. The next issue will be edited by Kelvin Corcoran.

This issue has been set in Bembo with titling in Argumentum.
The flyleaf is set in Trend Sans.

Contents

Mark Dickinson	5
Frances Presley	11
Peter Robinson	18
Alexandra Sashe	24
James Bell	28
Michelle Penn	31
Julie Irigaray	34
Peter Larkin	37
Kate Miller	40
Khaled Hakim	43
Julie Sampson	48
John Levy	52
Makyla Curtis	58
Rosanna Licari	60
Ann Matthews	62
David Miller	64
Caroline Hawkridge	66
Dikra Ridha	69
Marianne Burton	74
Steve Spence	76
Jennifer Spector	80
Sarah James	83
Nathan Shepherdson	85
Colin Campbell Robinson	88
Dennis Barone	92
Elżbieta Wójcik-Leese	95

Masayo Gôshi (*translated from Japanese by the author*) 97
Szymon Słomczyński (*translated from Polish by Elżbieta Wójcik-Leese*) 101
Menno Wigman (*translated from Dutch by Judith Wilkinson*) 102

Notes on Contributors 105

Mark Dickinson

Olav's Wood

We sought love among those narrow trails,
the lived light curving between the glittering
wood moss, and the wind burnt wynds where patience
grew selective through a force that gathered
to a common feather, touching the lifting
feature of how we came to the touch
of a frizzled pincushion. Becoming a gift
where we would dwell, knowing the Holarctic
elegance colonising the duration
of what we felt, and sought at the threshold
slant to the water. Estranging bitter/
interruptions lifted from the dazzling
frown, notched to a distant twist of cruelty
that violence heats. At the side, we stopped:

before a silken retreat, where the water
of the burn/ split into the silver
carpet of a woven orb/ rhizoid
tapestry drawn to its shade, among tea-
pots nesting— sung to the heart, where the fragile
laughter's treading the love to the audible
Crake, blessed in the slant/ light that implicates
faith, and greets us, inclining the elegant
bristle among the spring that counts the syl-
lables of discovery. Feeling the earth
in the glittering slants, which fade down in-
to the comforting hint of a beauteous
narrow, whose star water carries the softest
notes of happiness, to harmonise the tree
side of this temple where the world grows
                              better than
                                  before.

Angelic (kneads) Umbellifer

Shrunk to its need, the hybridity of wild encasing through gift those specular intervals of nodal foreshortening to the secular kneads of ground; low distancing, between leaf nodes and the dense splay of the crown. Where the leafy chlorophyll crouched to resistance, diverts to a thickness of grace. Couched along latitudes, each cell of nurture stems the over-reach to a thicknesses apex. Restraining the upright through a cleft of occupancy, where risks of height sway before prostrate increments of impotence. Such potent respite before a paradigm will opportune in the store of density, recoverable in this open extremity. Aligned to succession/ compressed to a hollow, where depth retains hereditary postures within a reach specific to its niche. Hunkering fit withstanding the jettisoned from opened drops of ocean-sharp, bitten-at-sore. Graft to its draft, each leafy dimension marks visible the open constraint: imparts within the bounded condition the measure of restraint. Any faint stands will at loss, as any over-height of obduracy frails upon florescence. Such stranding makes in its specular increments the standing on offer, lessening by trials beside a trail on this coastal way. Salt dash galing that moderates the song of its outburst, raising the annuity, razing the quiet solemnity; kneading the futures given to porrection to see what gives. Fleshing site-base, with a slope-flush of promise; shifting maritime climax with pronounced fluctuations in the northern range. Windbelt to over-arching—supine: therophyte generating radical inheritance, whose continuity is the measure of concentrated patience? Saline pin-point marks the offer, locating modified rations to its shore, and makes between the morphological strands, conditions for angelic stands.

Low (leaves) Moment

i

I do not fully understand
these leaves and their low moment of inertia
or the pattern of veins and the tiny bones
fitted with the impulse to travel;
there simply isn't enough
sunshine, (gas exchange or light capture)
entering through the open stomata,
knowing the warning signs
but editing the pain.

I've become accepting of inhumanity
schooled by the market
through the nerves that travel to the brain.
The surface morphology is mostly quiet
and the mechanical motion which, could be useful
to the superhydrophobic structure
concerned with the properties of men,
quickly grows in an uncertain ratio
attempting to think the essence of god.

ii

In the winter when the tree was tree-less
I remembered the aggregates and the photogenic quality of the larynx,
and in grouping the object similarities of our orifices,
I note the pitted lenticels
while failing to note the age of each clone.
Perhaps in the new light of tomorrow
my thoughts won't echo
and the world and its layers
will no longer be recognisable.

Today, I dug in the rain again and watched the deductive system
with impotence, neither bothered about the caustic nature of lime
or the continuity of each individual mix.
I changed my mind, but couldn't change my circumstance.
This demonstration of the gap between
that happened when the ear was windowless,
I read as a combination of micro and nano structures,
established in the early developmental stages
that remained specifically dependent on the reader's own position.

iii

There are many ghosts
and many recognitions,
in the valley crossing itself, I wait alone
among the litter, another
northern sound on the edge
of the moor; dwelling in humiliations
aimed at my weakness, that represent
the trade of Freud and the degrees
of separation in the historical hour of this personal damp.

Where I have leaves, white into the dark
goes echoing some familiars, fluttering like
the twinkling flat of an angle, that almost
to silence—silence backs to its origin
stemmed from a quaking whisper
to the vertical cells; I to its slights of separation
into chambers between, where we feel the days
and the venation in parallels leaves
into the open space to pore the light.

iv

Softly now, without disinterest avowing the refuge of
stone, but cautious of the limit crossing between
decisions, liberating the gift from beneath the wavy divide
among the saproxylic insects, guided through
the negative shadow to the outer side of being,
that we admit to absolutely, or, not at all. Out
in the garden, the dioecious sphere corrected
by neutrality—such remains the question
bordered by the thinnest of moss which edges this deep.

I to its wish, stays sudden, strays tranquil/ weeping Aspen's—
to a Lichen of cover, patterned by thoughts made angular
among the pieces of starlit catkins and the tiny seed
floating down from a crown that zones the mystery,
back to the question that is not self-evident, which
walks controversially in the salted turbulence
that scorch the edges of skin, where the sky
looks wet near the flexible leaf blade, piercing
estrangement through the passion of alternatives.

Envisaged by the visible that's dispossessed from the collar of liquidation—how does the word in its silence pierce the open battered by indefinite chatter?

Frances Presley

punch holes

        I lift my conditional arm

       move forward

        look for

                [   ]

       I lift my conditional arm

      move forward

       look for

                [a decision space]

         move forward

wings

> *I think of writing a book of Flyology*
> A. A. Byron, age 13, 1828

I am going to take the exact pattern of a bird's wing
            [exact]   [bird]

I have already thought of a way of fixing them on to the shoulders
                            [fix]

a pair of paper wings in proportion to my size
                            [my size]

they might be made of oil silk   try what I can do with feathers
          [made]   [do]

I can find no difficulty   in the motion   or distention of the wings
     [no]   [motion]

to move an immense pair of wings   take an airswallowing

      jet engine
                            downstream wakes
                                    [wakes]

to put serrations on the trailing edge   tattered fringe of a scarf

      fringe feathers break up   sound waves
                                                [waves]

     velvety down feathers absorb noise above 2,000 hertz

or change the angle at which air flows

        silent brush   of a Critch-owl's wing
        [silent]   [wing]

    velvet coating on the landing gear

thrush

I fear it is a London Bird. But something better than a sparrow too
  [fear it is]   [something better]

        The Bird is let out of her cage every morning
                    [let out]

She is very tame altho' of a species inclined to flights & migration
                                          [flight]   [migration]

I saw 50 thrushes in 2 low cages   for sale   in Churn Passage
 [I saw 01   thrush]   [rummage]   [Stonenest Street]

      & they have so haunted my imagination
      [& they]   [dark spots in my eyes]

I am dying from a pain of thrushes
            [from a crying]   quitquiquit   quitquiquit

crow

She wants to fly into ou neck & nestle up to ou
       [fly into]   [&]

    Ou won't hurt her I think, will ou?
        [hurt her]

He is a good crow
   [good]

        (tho' he does try to murder his thrush now & then)
            [murder his]   [now & then]

2

I want you to bike with me to Cockshoot Broad
    [want you]   [with me]

we enter a bird hide & startle a large black crow
    [enter]   [hide]

                doesn't seem to know how to get out
                    [seem to know]

clings to the wooden slats
    waddles on the floor   an old woman

we sit very still
    [sit]   [still]

crow finds the gap and stumbles out
    [find]   [out]

                flies straight up and away
                    [straight]   [away]

we say Nevermore to each other
    [say]   [each other]

How can a bird hide in a bird hide?   How can it be designed?

        [hide]   [bird]   [design]

Note

Ada Lovelace, or Ada Byron before her marriage to William King, Earl of Lovelace, studied the theory of flight when she was thirteen. Throughout her life she loved birds, especially song birds, and identified with them, giving bird names to herself and close family. Flight from her mother, and later her husband, were never far from her mind. I have designed these poems to 'show through' key words which could be revealed by a punch card: each word or phrase is a hole created by the programmer and known as a decision space. Ada wrote about the prototype of the computer, Charles Babbage's Analytic Engine, with its Jacquard loom punch cards. She also realised its potential for uses beyond the purely arithmetical.

Peter Robinson

Ravishing Europa

for O

After staying up far too late
for a televised debate
and sickened by their bickering,
I'm reminded of Europa
by yet more mendacious bullshit –
but gone to bed, succumb
again to sorry memories …
They bring back lying with the victim
of a far-off rape, a
ravishing, like the ones depicted
in occidental summer twilight
on these sunset lands.

Now you haver round our bedroom.
Me, I'm undecided whether
it had been an act of love
or violence provided
the very idea, to try the patience
of Europa, send her home …
But no, deciding for us
despite the Cretan myths, the liars,
here you are beside me –
and I can only hope
it's like we're in the arms of Europe
with Europe in my arms.

Lincolnshire Landscapes

for Peter Makin

'... there is a constant sense, as in a Dutch landscape,
of how the road leads on beyond the visible horizon.'
Richard Wollheim

1

Farmed deer – they're venison under rain –
bound off on balletic points;
but we're about to lose our way
with a box-pew church ahead,
its east end silhouetted
up against rain-laden sky –
the pockmarked, ochre stonework bitten
in by centuries of frost.

2

Under big skies of the Lincolnshire Wolds
when driven down field-skirting roads,
I'm grateful for that constant sense
of how they lead beyond
the visible horizon, land
moved across our windscreen frame,
our windscreen smeared by summer's extinctions;
it's shot through with reflections
overlaid experience
like sands rippling along a shore ...

3

the shore at Mablethorpe, for instance,
with its razor-shells, hundreds and thousands,
and wind, wind speaking in tongues
of streaming sands –
wraiths blown towards a steely sea
break, break, breaking under iron-grey cloud forms,
where figures, patterns on that beach,
point off towards more ghost propellers
over beyond the Wash, you see,
or Humber estuary.

4

Leaving the big red VOTE LEAVE signs
behind us in a homing turn,
we find the B-roads lead beyond
where abandonment, abjection, it will have them choose;
it's figured in those FOR SALE boards,
and what of language, person, coast
emerges now we are to lose
ourselves beyond the turning lines
from a lost horizon …

Garden Thoughts

'mi pareva di essere in Europa'
Luciano Erba

At this hour they may well be
watering gardens throughout Europe,
but beyond the misted window
our front-garden patch
has an air of strangeness (though
Japanese anemones,
foxglove bells and fuchsias
hedged round by the box in disarray
could be thus any year);

now in this miserable June
when the dwarf pine thrusts up taller
and a tumbling acer
fills out its underskirts,
raindrops flicker in the puddles
adding globules and a gleam
to droop-headed flowers –
like they too want their country back,
and it's not coming home.

Bibliographical Note

'Es war ein Traum.'
Heinrich Heine

for Derek Slade

I dreamed last night, or the night before,
how something of mine
unexpectedly appeared in a little magazine
whose pages fell out on the floor –

for this publication had the strangest of styles:
its format's ragged margin
formed the whole coastline
of the British Isles.

24 August 2016

In the Apennines

after Eric Newby

Even the sunflowers look depressed
as we drive towards those hills –
heads bent, desiccated, no longer turn
petals crazed with light to any sun.
Our talk, too, touches on downturns
in the market price for wheat
now this region's pasta-making firms
don't buy local either.

Yet eyes gaze still to the fields of hill farms,
their turned earth dry, as low sun warms
familiar curves, and the holiday
season brings our families out to eat
grilled meat in the mountains.

Precipitous views to far crests would start
ever more distant memories
of things dads' said about those years:
what happened at Torrechiara
or Berchetto, where the Germans were,
and a granddad in black-tasselled fez
among the disappeared …

But now sky softens to a cloud-flecked blue,
I think of you hidden from war's alarms,
harms, and excursions hereabouts,
who came back after to find your love
and did, and married her –

think of that, here, as, relaxed outside,
we've formed a wider family circle
and the recent generation's
minx-like three-year-old daughter runs
now to one, now another's arms.

Alexandra Sashe

the last homage to Paul Celan

From the letter, inanimate
– my orphan, his anima –
half-path between
grass and hay :
half-feathered, half-weathered
half-buried and half-winged

a lapis lazuli opens the space,
    the king of his own letter
bequeaths his language : his pain and
his secret –
    a portion of each
    he takes

    into the river.

The Square is freed from the name of the tree
it served not, –
and keeps its leaf
  dry and hidden
among the pages that speak of the king :

who speaks
 through his thirst
his hunger.

    Our
    hands navigate through the river.
    Our breaths live.

Two poems from the cycle Landescapes

The small, the hidden, the bluebell words
of the Fatherland, written
in harsh, in milk
upon the skin, the veins, the stencil lines
of my palms.

I have ploughed the thought of the Land,
have brought
the rugged, the furrowed, to white
to smooth, to a clean
paper.

     I have washed the sky
     and erased the night,
from my sleep, my sleepless, my walk
to the temple.

I have learnt a motionless time, –
and drink
from the sole unsinkable
confident flight
of a morning owl.

§

The rain divided the Land
the avid mouth, the numb
thirst of the earth. –
                            With clean and faultless
                    wounded hands is received, the rain.

We have ploughed the sky with our eyes,
with our earthy pardons of hearts'
droughts. –
                        With a grey
                forbearance of the clouds
                washed and received we are, in the rain.

At the churchyard are found names,
a blessed absence, its truth and fullness. –
All the knowing is kneeling
                    and offers its sleepless bed
for the earth of the flowerbed
and a bluebell.

from the cycle Situations of the Wind

This lake is a secret impossibility
a one-shore soleness
cognate to eye.

A plexus of focal distances
that justifies its surface.

    Bells wash their evening sounds.
    Echoes sink, and the carillon gives
    each one apiece
    a viatical blessing.

The disburdened birds return at the lake
    – the tree is their crown and sister – and
they believe in its waters.

They know of an unattainable height
of the eyes that dwell
above the tower.

At dawn they weave
of leaves and feathers
          a nest
                pure of purpose and calling. –
With every strike of the morning bell
they deny
  themselves
above the lake surface.

James Bell

the words remain the same

the old stones never collect moss though
are wind carved
               collect centuries instead
imply design and hieroglyphs that grow
from maps –
               notice a menhir not marked

the one beside the wayside calvary –
an oversight
               a cartographic glitch that

years will repair – see Porzic is there
remember it
               scribed a corn circle – an alien
outline in undulations of the wheat –
next year grass
               the marker of stone remains

Cailovan needs to be looked for – rests
proud meadowed
               on its hillock beside a stream

stone and water always last longer – hide
their history
               well enough behind words

matter in their own terms of time – can never
collect moss
               or sway sound like a wind chime

each opposite tumuli are stone bards with
songs chilled
        under questions in summer heat

the words remain the same – makars make
interpretations
        tunes turn in their own patterns

from the lowlands

sine yin cuttance currie-wurrie
        in this a disputed account
wi ane fung hunch
        with a shoulder shove
lummed ramage
        wild and untamed
wi rizzon or nane
        with or without reason
fir stammygaster
        for an unpleasant surprise
sinder frae mistrow
        and part with disbelief
tae spae yir girth
        foretell your place of sanctuary
gang oan lika tume
        chatter on without pause
gilradge eneuch
        and make merry enough
ilka thrawn chile
        every ill-natured person
whae gange laib
        who talks insolently
tae ae scurrent ambaxiator
        to a disgusted ambassador

aneath usquebae
        controlled by whisky
ilka capernicious capercailzie
        each short tempered grouse
lamwart bred
        uncouth from the country
tae halfhede brindle
        to the temple of money
orra rage gadgie
        strange mad fellows
whay spak brilzeans
        who speak nonsense words
lowden louthers
        amongst subdued and idle loiters
hail eldritch
        wholly unearthly

Michelle Penn

The Japanese Vase

Repair should be evident. It should strut an arrogant song, instead of pacifying quietly. It should deny nothing.

She has never restored a single ceramic by hiding the cracks, the chips, replenishing patterns exactly where their colours have strayed. Her sutures show, a defiant testament to damage. The withered fingers lay down gold lacquer, honouring every imperfection, every beautiful break. One scarred lover caressing another.

Repair bellows. It is not a bird, pecking seeds from a child's hand. It is not the woman who trades all she is for costume jewellery.

She is in love with the unused vase on the table, so exposed outside its shelter of Styrofoam. It begs for the strength she will someday bestow, its surface so intact, so ignorant of history.

A Transplant Surgeon's Apology

                                      The needle
wisped,
       blunt eyelash

             broaching your deepest root, the you
      you will never see
In and out—

                                      Perhaps I am
a sinner
       coupling unlikes

             transgressing
      the inviolate vessels
one to one, one

loop, another—
                                      God in the needle's mouth.

                                      Perhaps I am
a vandal
       wielding the blade

       inflicting damage
       to negate a greater damage

replacing what nature gave

                                      Perhaps I am
an artist

    plying
    my materials:

        capillary, fascia,
            muscle, to the finest knot—

I apologise for this intimacy.

I am no lover, no
        philosopher, my
        cool glove probing
            the substance of your hope.

Julie Irigaray

The Fall of the West

Comfortable bubbles of barbed wires:
Refugees are refused the land beyond.

Concrete rabbit-cages reaching the sky:
Ghettos with curfew, fertile ground for fanatics.

"We are a free country":
Modernity as an omnipotent god.

Defenders of our superiority:
Inquisitors tracking behind the beard and the veil.

Al-Andalus swapped for the crusades:
The hand of Fatima is the new yellow star.

"They brought the plague to our civilization":
Cholera was already gangrening it.

"A nation is a race":
Some seek for an expulsion via the ballot paper.

The world post nine-eleven carries on
The traditions of the old wars of religion.

My generation will never remember
How life was before the fall –

Fall of man, fall of the empire,
Fall of Granada, fall of the towers.

There is no *shalom* for *Inch Allah,*
No taste of pistachio in our speech any longer.

Juliet's Chest

This town's typical
        rosé marble
aggressed me
        with its umbilical
        memories:

        a fuchsia ray
was projected
        for Pink October
on Verona's eroded arena
– another tragic opera.

Women handed out
        moon roses
but I wasn't ready to let
        them pin ribbons
        on my chest –

        ★

Six months later I returned
        there with my mother
to celebrate my birthday,
        or her first fight with flesh.

Her cherry cheeks sweat
        like a glass under the zenith,
her magenta top contrasted
        with her widow's fan
and her topknot was a proud rooster.

She didn't wear a turban
        as when she'd fought
the spider weaving an irradiated
        cobweb in her chest.

        ★

We visited the sham house of Juliet Capulet:
her bronze statue stood in the courtyard

where voyeurs deflowered
her tarnished breast –

Replicas of her boobs were sold
as vulgar fetishes.

They looked like cheap amulets
against breast cancer.

Voodoo Dolls

I've found your Amerindian match box
with a woven poncho on the cover.
I was baffled by this hued sarcophagus:
Maya mummies with hampered legs
and lucky charm beans were entombed in it.

The two voodoo dolls wore class
photo close-ups as death masks.
You repeated you'd never use black magic,
yet you caught a hatred spell on the evil
spirits who persecuted you at school.

Bad memories must be erased
to set you free, my river deity.
I placed them in the sand bag I gave you
with two pebbles picked along the shore
and the shells you collected for me.

I threw it away from the bridge you jumped off
and watched it sinking with a feeling of accomplishment.

Peter Larkin

Emergent Habits: Nearest Dress Far Over Trees

Emergent habits
from counter-habitual,
dressed for unfamiliars
one more attiring

                                   the cocoon of outspread
                                   quickens a loosened
                                   unloser, throw
                                   a scarf's

how a scurf of trees
extenuates, tempers
the emergence

                              clothes us in frail fabrics
                              unscrambling horizon
                              with seeing scars,
                              a thatch of spars
                              below their watch
                              of semi-stars

lagging ahead of the mut-
ilated, fostered to its
crooks, gives replenishment
shawl by shawl

                              no tree simulacra
                   inciting the swerve from field,
                       veteran neck turns in-
                         ordinately round scarf:
                       bypassing the cycle gives
                         emergent nub, one offer
                           on from saturate hub

not always succinct in adhesion, a capacity poor-store bare enough
for the jolt of emergence   dresses then what had lost its way from
floor   whichever root-bound knows no more branch-zero   re-
bestirs a post-avoidance, the layer itself was already speculative

too slight along to have
rested at a blunt touch,
a sheering of counter-shoot
but stunted (sprinted)
by invasive variation
at the consentive spark

                          lapsed overheads dilate
                     a throw's declination, bring
                       uprights their preferences
                         in stubbing   imparted
                       back to shelter, such thin
                            permissions stray
                            to the commutatory

the least glut is some
misfeed foraged towards:
a tree before its scarf not
so much draped as dropped
on a designatory   benign
baffle as inceptional sock
coats the annexation

                                                    scarce crumbs of nature
                                                    at its horde's seasonal
                                                    office of not now
                                                    crowding out
                                                    the canopy of prayer

not treelessly put to the edge of
copse, erring from stand to
grove, from canopy to ambient
blowing scarf   where
the shocks of emergence
leave a cluster

a leaf one of its selves towards a wave of scarf, not yet a leash of fabric
no secular clump gathers this emergent profile   the oak's sediment
ripped from hierarchy, wrap *that* in the scarf's flare   wading an
emergence dries towards waddage, slowly to irrigations of prayer

                                                    pray across the unshadowed,
                                                    what a texture of tree-dress
                                                    (penetration's duress) won't
                                                    have had to thin out to

amplified remotely, in-
timately comparisoned shoot
over root   such caparisons
thread the emergence,
embed symmetrical
resurgents

Kate Miller

The Locomotion of Laundry

All things began in order, so shall they end and so shall they begin again
        Sir Thomas Browne

Always on the move: outlawed, bundled,
sheets straggle, deep in wait for their ablution, taps to open,
washer drum to turn.
                Cloth which wound around the living
– and preserved the record in its creases –
only had to flop down on the floor
to forgo the old life.
                        But there's no hurry.
Everything is taken up and everything descends,
tugged from the rubber cervix, treated to a midwife's slap,
                each coming newly into
                                being at the separation.
In the tango of its hanging,
        a shirt or bedding that until this morning bore
another body's trace,
takes up position as a fighter, felon, dancer, tackler, striker,
                                airblown along the line.
There may be occasional arrests
                        yet piece by piece,
by pawn-like moves they are reshaped,
redeemed in the perpetual lifting and laying-on of hands
and so *shall they begin again*, to enter every room.

The term Locomotion *was coined by Sir Thomas Browne*

From Seed

Your cousins sent a handful in a twist of bubble-wrap
the Autumn you were born.
The second Spring I noticed one
self sown:
        because it meant to stand its ground,
        stay put, as any small child would, this acorn
        anchored up and down in earth,
        through earth, by sticking out

two tongues of growth from tarnished halves of brass.

Antenna
poking from the grass
became the first line of a tree – lengthening –
the hedgers' *whip* or sapling,
upright and thin,

        gaining in girth ... until the end
        of a fifth winter when twigs began
        to open to the sky from fists of buds, hands
        gloved, sporting mussel-orange cuffs of curly leaves.

Twenty years it takes until a new oak sets
its maiden crop and maybe twenty more before the seed is good.

        One year when you're grown
        you'll roll a clutch of green-skinned acorns,
        phials in your palm,
        and wonder what may come of them.

Each little armoured cap contains
contradicting offers
to the touch:

the dimpling of a thimble
and the stubby pin of a grenade:
made to cradle and release
a small smooth head.

Khaled Hakim

Letter from the Takeaway (3)

I keep dreming ive got a term project where ive never gon back to the class in months.

Yoo imagin inconseqwensial hermeticks abandoning th masses; you never interview anywon less than a rap gangsta, defens lawyer with a film deal, riting not narativ

In several yers nothing makes a diffrens. Animus ingested entropy remaines. Reserchers in a pharmaseutical discover a receptor for Republicanism in the brain.

Wher is it situated a poem impossibl to acsess. Experiens tels me noone wil giv a living riting word salads, I wudnt bet on riting not narative

but how do ye *kno* an audiens cant get it. Ive ever made judgments on behaf of peple.

A polemick of use value. Storiz setling unstably between textuality & inertia

eliptical poetris of a clozd univers, suckd back to th pointles event horizon of my arsehol:

I got my langwage from a sawcer loopy consummat stylist of th new phyzics. Its such a relief to find discours owtside of discorse, hyperbolick retoricks of openess held in check by engineering

altho matter everywere pul on it, spred thin enufh so that it wil never collaps back onto anything important

'I' as emergent phenomenon, imperial syntax – yor emergent behaviour

w/ time they al fade toward invizibility, thir shop sine radiacion geting weker & weeker – the parabolick bearly making it to infinity bcfor exhawsting kinetic energy, to end as a tandoori cinder

declarativs of the new natur, omniscient descriptiv of a universal discors nowon knos wat theyr tawking about

geometrick waves dizolving ripple molds on the clozd I

the order of development, zygotes pulsing, genoms turning eche other on & off on the bullion network

eche lihtbulb connected to 2 others switching faster than liht chasing informasion beyond the 'C' of relativitie in a cyberloop flying sauser

antichaos boxes its possibilitees into a tiny range as shit fals on the shitpile model, landslides bild to stabl states, to periodic tectonick colapse, we only hav won pile of shit afeckting eny part of th pile

systems permanent wobble between redundancie & automatizm, grammar pressurs default

an expected property of mathematical chemicals

proze autocatalytic sets, intrinsic dynamicks of probubble structur

celular automata dying, expanding paradym loops from a sentral region ded tree – expanding *what*?

ther ar only 2 rules – Reproduce – Mutate

the parasites take advantige of information, others take advantage of th parasites, & others cheet on society, wether chemistri of carbon & hydrogen, or the computer bits simulacion of Hegelian society

logickless currency fluctuacions of democratick capitalizm, the end of th best of worlds - the prosodic tools predictiv power

look for paterns & price fluctuacion, understand L=A=N=G=W=I=G=E poeticks, make a fortune on stocks & shaers

eny ecosystem exists at khaos antikhaos –

whas a chronometer – 2 snails placd on a copper plate forever in sympathetik communicasion

the oscilating energy of sparks as electromagnetick waves as lipodes spred owt on a pond

whoever hears it coms into tune, the amplitud is magnifiyd

The Hertz transcever acros a tiny gap iz this letter, mor vigorus sparks of a sensless devise

wave a white handkerchief ech time the recever experiment fail

informasion collects in the medium sieve providense, random karma colects structur poetick merits

awtomatizm from the remote generacion, err...extempore orders the poem only poetrie az far as its prose

defining featur prosodic chaos, the simple

Medical orderlis kno the bacilli warfare woond infection from Boer bullets

from yor serch for th magick bullet, the cure for syphilus in rabbits (compound 606); the protozoa in retreet: many mor babies went home with thcr motherz to becom a burden on homeostasis

apoptosis cels in the embryos hand die off to sculpt personal lifstyls, canser stains delectable expressionizm

stress levels decline, cemical balans describe wizdom, cells being told to die

odor stains knit cloze together, charity shops subsidizd purpos

dependansy infrastructurs graduat reserch its hundred thousand culturs in robot assembly – suported by corporat hardframe

litle I, th valorizd underclas in universitie, trying to rite the cliche & unspekable

O Planet of the Lower Classes

ware litle white daddyz girls opress the blak studs – now *hoo* am i thinking of ther

suppresst in liberal storiz of essentialist conflict

empowerment by predacion – *Stab up me meat, boy, stab up me meat*

batty bwoys getting ther hed mashd in by gobshite w/ hihly developd sense of black potency, & blordclaat sociology

I dont speke worrd a man – dis sey I must mooltiplie, an mankind unto mankind is an abominacion heh heh heh

political definicions pop – all Black peple ar interreplasable, therfore I only need one homogeneus black blob

The desert iland test of the ontogenetick.

Langwige defining geografies waer the universals of anthropologie play owt the constant oposition – defining 'selfhood' in th tribe, the conservativ economy of identitie

Oh God – Im a racist! God, wharra releef.

at 10-43 second, temperatur a funcsion of overcrowding 1032 degrees, the 4 nown forsez of aire fyre curry powder & water wer one

the eliptical model poem has a begining end a liftime. Gravitacional redundansy is relentless. Its contents ar destind to fry.

Julie Sampson

South-West's Sea Thyme

i.m. H.D. (Hilda Doolittle) who lived in Devon and Dorset, in 1916, & Cornwall, in 1918

Does a poet, stretching time, see way ahead of her the backflow of tide and so intuit, in sea-breaths a future leaning back toward her, slowly, irrevocably, keening her in?

Driftwood

    Breathless, at last
we are here, at the sea-shrine,
though few seem to venture
to this abandoned plot, where
at the time of the latest tide
       a twist of drift left
behind figures
    for us,
the gravitational curve,
   a centenary – the sea's-time.

                   'you are useless, O grave, O beautiful'
                          (The Shrine)

Sea-Blackthorn (Sea-Berry)

We are stung by salt-
in-tide from the now
looming beach
      a windbreak,
this shrub is spiny,
   has thorns, yet our way
is strewn with a sea-gift
greeting – the little orange-tree –

its cluster of golden fruit –
(or is the gold-rush not
   for us – is it then, instead,
      our perfidious bliss?)

> *'pour meted words / of sea-hawks and gulls /*
> *and sea-birds that cry / discord'*
> *(The Wind Sleepers)*

Sea-Thrift

      Flowers flung in Devon's cliff-crevices
rock-rose cradled
      within these veil-protecting drifts –
your rosette language will
      be secreted, caught in the sap
of deep under-roots' ascent
through tensile stems and flowers
          dispersing honey-sweet,
    Heaven-sent
        air.

> *'more precious / than a wet rose /*
> *single on a stem / – you are caught in the drift.'*
> *(Sea Rose)*

Only we were left

      at the place near where river meets estuary,
         not far from the pebble-beach.

Here, as at any place (even at the murmurating coast)
      things aren't always as they seem –
our way is hemmed with the green fringe of Alexanders,
shoots already dashed with early tale-tale yellow dye

whilst a scatter of solitary egrets flush Otter's river
and reed-beds with fleeting icons
    of white –

      but also, we know,
that somewhere along river's elongated reach
unsettled beaver kits rudder through water to their lodge
      hidden deep beneath
      and   there! –
we hear a bloodcurdling cry from high
behind already raucous rookery pines.

I'm reminded of love and legend,
    in some places
    Umbelliferae
    are designated
    Mother! Die!
Beware, don't pick these plants they say,
(perhaps confused with the perils of Hemlock).

    No, not all is at it might seem –
      so few of us left to heed
at the place where river and nearby estuary meet.

        'And the marsh dragged one back/
        and another perished under the cliff/
        and the tide swept you out'
            (Loss)

At the Fort; The Beacon, Martinhoe

We arrive from the old Roman carriageway
    high
above the sea, next the sky,

      way below
in coastal chasms, white against white

   gannets and gulls
       beating,
             breaking surf –

  at home
our multimedia screens still on
flashing in-perpetuum into our comfort-zone rooms,
every opportunity, we whip out phones from pockets or bags,
photos flash, burst from our finger-tips –
we remain alive with interactive possibility,
yet find it impossible to conjure a picture from the swiftly lit
spark of a stated fact.

Here   only flashes, a series of dots and dashes
cracking along faults of the rocky screes on this north Devon coast
from long-ago beacon fires
intended for those, rudderless,
tossed in the turbulent sea,
             waiting,
   in the Channel,
watching for life or death landings.

> *'I have stood on your portal/and I know-/*
> *you are further than this, still further on another cliff'*
> *(Cliff-Temple)*

Does a woman, growing older, (rubato – rallentando), slowly holding back those years before her, re-memorise unrealised moments in quickening lost time behind, whilst the irrevocable in-rush of waves threaten to engulf – take her?

Note: quotations following each poem
are from H.D.'s poems, in *Sea-Garden*

John Levy

Some of What I've Lost

I lost out, I
lost in, I lost over and through and am not
sure how to lose from. I lost the foreheads of my
late parents along with the rest of their

physical presences. I lost the voices of my
late parents along with the chance to call them
long distance when I wasn't in Phoenix. I
lost, because I never had it, the idea that I could ever

understand what made another person tick and
I never understood how another person could be like
a clock's innards. I lost the shoe I had
before we moved from Minneapolis and I liked not

wearing the shoe more than wearing it because
when it was off I could see on the circular label
Buster Brown and his presence was a comfort,
a friend in another place like a

pen pal except I was too young to write letters
or know what a pen pal was. I lost the tree
outside my second floor childhood window
in Minneapolis the big one

I used to watch fill slowly with
blue then deeper blue and purpling dusk that
would fill the tree between the branches between the leaves
and as it did that wide

tall tree filled me with blue then deeper blue and purpling.
I lost my favorite piece of white string I carried around all week
one summer. I lost each and every silver-colored cap gun
I shot, smelling the gunpowder. I lost the fear and hatred

of the words dick and cock that I had in fourth grade and
in the Madison Meadows locker room
when I heard Paul say *penis* unlike all the other kids I knew Paul
was going to be my friend and I was right for

a few decades at least. I lost a poem I thought I'd love
when I read in a Table of Contents DEFINITION OF MELODY
and eagerly turned to it and found
DEFINITIONS FOR MENDY, a poem

I then did read but I lost the poem I thought I'd find.
I lost the fear of someone killing me
by putting ground glass into my food a fear I had after
watching a show (Alfred Hitchcock?) on which

that's how a person was slowly done in. I lost the fear
I had of my silverware turning against me if I didn't
treat it right at every meal and use the spoon as much
and as gratefully as the fork. I lost any chance

that this poem could be revised into
a haiku. I lost every flat rock that I skipped across
a body of water hoping the skipping would last longer.
I lost the belief that anyone over 18 was in the world

of grown-ups. I lost control just now
when I wanted to use the word *un-childish*, but without
a hyphen, and my computer changed it (because I didn't
insert a hyphen) into *enchiladas*. I lost for the moment all

three of my different books of Frank O'Hara poems though I know I'll locate One soon and making that O upper case is just a way of paying respect to O'Hara. I lost and frequently lose solitude and regain it and lose it and am glad about both the losses

and gains. I lost the opportunity and an opportunity and so many opportunities and don't know how I could ever decide which is *the* opportunity I most regret losing. I lost the opportunity to address you as *Dear Reader* anywhere until now.

(Death) Death (Death)

(1)

death disguised as nothing ever after

night

(2)

I ask Alan about death
he answers, *death is just death*

I didn't meet him until we were both safely out
of our childhoods although I can't speak for him and
I am not sure I can say I have ever been
safely
out

(3)

William Carlos Williams came to me out of his *Selected Poems* one Saturday when I was 15 in Walden Books, alone, reading from A to Z on the poetry shelves waiting to decide – over two Saturdays of reading at least one poem per book in the hundreds of them, holding on to my two bucks and waiting until I'd finished to decide what I most wanted to own and then reading Williams and knowing. I walked home with his book, stopping on an empty street after rereading his poem about a cat stepping down into an empty flower pot and a black cat on the street in front of me crossed my path with Williams' cat in my mind and that black one flowed.

(4)

where does death fit in

I hate to think of death "fitting in"

(5)

the first poem in his *Selected* that I read was
"The Widow's Lament in Springtime"
and that
did it

then I found the cat in a poem titled "Poem" and

(6)

I haven't talked about his face
on the black-and-white cover of his *Selected* how
he looked, to me at 15, so
almost mild, so unposed, so just
there, like a guy who could be standing behind me
in line to buy a book in that store, an old guy
wearing glasses

William Carlos Williams

the cat
climbed over
the top of

the jamcloset
first the right
forefoot

I didn't even think

"what *is*
a jamcloset?"

(7)

I saw the cat
descending

ending

in the pit of the empty
flowerpot

where I now think we all
end up

along with everywhere else

Makyla Curtis

body atlas

I felt a pencil
in the small of my back –
a geographical alliance against the
outline coat of my body's consciousness.
The clutter is a casual start
with a clinical look at my journals
where the map spreads.
All lines are fingers against my figure sketched
my huffing remarks depart the record
the graph lowers, the arcing
centre line dips on the page
we, she and I, write into our ego a
bottle of scotch
place lucidity in a jar and
trace the outline of calligraphic memories.
The environment embellishes us
the small parts of my neck that
is a bump, a clumsy knot to the hand of a masseuse
tips the coastal line forming a bay
she, not she with me, she the masseuse
she rubs my asylum neck pushing it out
the study of my shoulder remains unchanged –
a case study of letters fixed into books,
old copperplate in every corner describing the whole
of me. An artwork. Some journey,
an incremental penholder is all.
the sleeves dribble like scribes and always
highly professional the tears in the map
run along the highly-used routes.
She, the she with me, lies with her back a ridge like mine
we are a mountain range, an alpine physique
with hands forming our own cartography.

Arum

They stand closely,
stamens, orange, in a sheathing bract.
I conflate. The tragedy in three, three skin pink,
is a story of solitary ambition
flat-footed frogs goading,
trading famous quotes for sanity.
A species of high-school cliques unfolds.
Flowers in Scotland become eyes backstage
gunpowdered and bloody
a sticking pin
between us like flowers, the play compounds
my adolescence in listing murders
for aggravated essays and dictation for
memorisation.
The familiar stamens flail in a
plot more dappled than spring.
Cleft leaves split and curl like tales.
The moss and beryl green cradles brass trumpets but the
throat like spathe dips white.
And we paint and paint, as small children we paint
the intricacies of white
reflecting refracting the adjacent.
The taxonomy of history
like a funnel
blames witches.

Rosanna Licari

The Hand

This is not usual.

The surgeon draws a Z with a pen to show where he will cut. The lump in the middle of my right palm protrudes like a limpet. It has grasped and fixed itself around the middle finger's tendon. The one that's strong as an octopus leg. Some have said it looks like a closed eye. Spooky. The doctor will join my heart, head and life lines and the receptionist vouches for his outstanding embroidery. In my mother's brain nothing is stitched together. Synapses collapse and don't form again. Neurons reach for what is left of sense, but meet nonsense. The obscure territories. Some have said the mad have the gift of prophecy. I tell Mother about the hand and she claims, *Yes, yes, I had this operation, too.* This is not fact. *Don't worry. It will all go well,* she continues. I take comfort in the assurance of a demented woman.

Wilpena Pound, the Flinders Ranges

The noise from the caravan park drifted into the desert and brushed against the ancient sandstone and quartzite. Adelaide was only hours away. In the morning, at the lookout, the range of mountains once mistaken for an old volcano, looked like a sunken cake. Everything was wrong, I was wrong. My face at your back, you'd stopped talking. At night, I dreamed of flying over this country. Wide expanses with purple hills and green stretches among the enduring red earth.

I was optimistic. I walked out into a flat, cloudless land that was clumped with grasses and low lying shrubs. Noise dimmed as I moved north and slammed into a terrain of deafening silence.

In the distance, an emu raced towards me. I stood very still. Then it stopped suddenly and ran towards the cabin. Inside, your crazy emu-eyes glared at me.

Ann Matthews

from Home Turf Sequence

*B*eing
the devil's
advocate can lead
you places that a*r*e sometimes
refreshing. M*y* favourite place is a home *n*ot
a building. I was in my Bront*e* phase that summer when I snuck out in my white ni*g*hty and wa*l*ked bare foot through the drenched grass and the candyfloss da*w*n mist. B*y* now Dover is almost a *s*econd ho*m*e. I'm not sure whether the sheep and ghosts of Tre Ceiri enjo*y*ed our version of free-jazz on saxop*ho*ne and tru*m*pet. *S*erial monogamy is a dirty occupation and not a label to be tagged with. I burnt my past, eight bin bags of writing, which turned into a *f*eathery pile *o*f ash, though some wo*r*ds *e*scaped and flutt*e*red o*v*er south Angles*e*y. Dad measured out pea*n*uts in identical eggcups and we *t*hought it best not to argu*e*. What is time but your measur*e*. This is the second recessio*n* that I have lived through but I can't distinguish a gap between them. Picking magic mushrooms on the school field was fun though I'd run awa*y* and curl up with a good book wh*e*n you consumed them. We seemed to follow the Fasching c*a*rnival from no*r*th to south Germany, beating out the winter in unison. Even nice people can be bad loser*s*. Thunder crashes once, light bulbs shatter and the green light screams like my sister. In the hot and tinder-dry bowl of the Hungarian plain herds of thin sheep bleated and undulating shoals of grey mice scattered. My subjectivity is part of who I am. I was fascinated by the intense lime-green and shiny finger-sized dips of the buttons on my cardigan.

from Home Turf Sequence

Week 5

...Patti S*m*ith beat her frail chest whilst she sang, Nic*o* cried *un*t*i*l her m*a*scara ran and dr*i*pped off her chi*n*, Cour*t*ney Love *th*rew out bottles of w*a*ter *t*o her gasp*i*ng fan*s*, Kim Gordo*n* lo*o*ked like an ice queen, Björk squatted on stage without apology and PJ Harvey crooned like Sinatra on speed. The *b*oot *i*s on a difficult foot and it hurts a *g*reat deal. There was an East Germany, a place that you entered with a visa, where old women dressed from head to foot in black and cackled with mirth when you fell over on the ice and landed on your arse. I desi*g*n in curv*e*s. It was the ene*r*gy vampires *tha*t did it – though I do*n*'t believe in them – the dog r*a*n home and a week later her name tag arrived in the post, found in a place we had never been to. I stood on the pavement balanced on one foot not knowing what to do – the ground was teeming with a carpet of ladybirds...

David Miller

from Epilogue

Two deer – a mother hind and her young – appeared in the garden, content to stand or sit in poses as if for lens, inked brush or pen, chewing foliage, even in the rain. For me, they were welcome, though you were apprehensive: rightly so, as later on they ate your roses, lilies and geraniums. As I walked along the arcade, a small horse came up behind me and put its forelegs on the back of my shoulders, licking my neck affectionately. I fell; the horse fell. The hedge sparrow flew at one of the glass walls and hit it; then fell, dazed, to the floor. I gingerly picked it up, feeling the softness of its body in my hands; when I set it down outside, the toes of one of its feet clung tenaciously to my finger. There: a swirl of blood across the grass; the mutilated carcass of a sheep. I threw the staff to the ground, breaking the ceremony, and abjured magic thenceforth. *And sometimes even the best captain loses his balance,* you wrote. Seagulls flew in circles in the darkening sky over a coastal village of white-painted buildings, with hills stretching beyond. *In all faces is seen the Face of faces, veiled, and in a riddle.* He wrote in praise of *the best nurses*, in a poem's dedication: the rest was dream and dreaming's release. He died in hospital; my other friend died in the sea. A necklace or chain thrown into the sky. A skirl. *By the way, you are first watch tonight. Close your eyes – and look at the schooner approaching.* Had you really listened to his music when you called him *a poor fool in the fullest sense of the word? Poor beyond all measure and foolish beyond all measure.* – And that day when you almost drowned, on the school trip to St Kilda Beach? – Yes, I was told to swim, without being asked if I *could* swim, and there was no question of querying the order; but it just seemed like one bad dream amongst others in those years. – Does it really shimmer, sway, surge, break? *…for the direct way to ascend is first to descend.* Spices, seeds, legumes, we used; and leaves, earth, wax, stones; also wool, calico, silk, cotton cloth; and doorframes, and sheets of glass. Snow blocks are placed in rows, forming a circle; then row piled upon row, with gaps filled with wedges of snow; the whole thing slanting towards a ceiling. Resist temptations to pour water on the exterior snow or light a fire inside.

> you could or you could
> not and would it
> be a pity
> steel bronze iron marble

A house made from boxes: wooden for the exterior, cardboard the interior. – It was the connection between poverty and art that concerned me, whatever the problems and contradictions; wanting an art that was pared down and without pomp or pretension or displays of sterile wit, and with common materials its basis. But not impoverished art, inane or trite art, or art for shock's-sake or as mere novelty. The written, the spoken: if a conflict then to no right end. The eye sees, the ear hears: first the lightning, then the thunder. Tap, tap, tap, tap: rain on window panes; and rain on plants in window boxes. – A kiss is a kiss unless it's a concept or a lie. Is a formality a concept? and does a lie always betray? The sky descends to the smallest flower: willingly, graciously.

> stars hill sea enfolded
> imprisoned or else released
> a lamp a table and wine
> window door gate and pathway

Elderberry dye soaks into linen. As the bridesmaid suffered from nosebleeds, her mother had brought along a supply of handkerchiefs in readiness. – Goodbye, the bride said to me, her young cousin, as she broke into tears: would we never meet again, I wondered? *Although it will most likely occur in the distant future, I would happily live to witness an exhibition of everything I have created and still hope to create, if only to arrive at the conclusion: is it anything and does it mean anything?* He told the man who'd gone blind to get down on his knees, and then he pissed into his eyes; and the man could see again.

Caroline Hawkridge

Sightings

*"Then felt I like some watcher of the skies
When a new planet swims into his ken..."*
                                        Keats

20-inch Uppsala Schmidt, Siding Spring Mountain.
  August 7th. McNaught, Robert H.
  75% various ices; the rest different dust.
  Inward bound towards perihelion.

It was hopelessly lost in December, but recovered
  in the deep twilight of the New Year.
  I will not soon forget this kernel of comet.
  First post on Yahoo! Duluth, Minnesota.

Most beautiful (and only) snowball I saw this winter.
  Today was 17° centigrade instead of zero
  but this melting dirty iceball in the universe
  has us happy, Davoko, Croatia.

I watched her for a long time in the company of a hunting hawk.
  McNaught in a flock of birds, Leszno, Poland.
  Even polluted Belgrade didn't stop her to shine.
  Wonderful decline of the day, Kiev, Ukraine.

Click to the left of the Statue of Liberty. Chinese 'broom star'.
  I climbed Stone Mountain to see it set against Atlanta.
  Upward tail indicates 'near pass', January 12th.
  Zodiacal light. A treat driving West.

Solar heat has puffed up the comet, causing it to brighten
    to a naked-eye object in broad daylight and blue skies.
    Somewhere over Bermuda out of our cockpit window.
    I saw it with a 64-year old's eyes.

23s exposure, then flash to light up the kids as it heads for the equator.
    Collisions with heavenly ice gave Earth vast amounts of water.
    Right ascension: celestial longitude through eastern Pegasus.
    Here, we cannot glance it.

Hurtling closer than Mercury to the sun, it could break up.
    Dust has been ejected before perihelion.
    The whole comet is my hand-span across.
    Its mammoth hair is way past Venus (smeared by solar wind).

We all rubbernecked a strange bushfire on the horizon;
    the reptile tongue of McNaught issuing from the veldt.
    A policeman reported a plane in trouble, trailing smoke.
    Many hundreds of people waited on the hills.

Nearly an hour after the comet dipped into the Pacific,
    we could still see the tail. Paranal, Atacama desert, Chile.
    Remnant streamers rose in San Francisco with the moon and Venus
    crowning us in the Alps after sundown, just like the white peacock

of de Cheseaux's comet in the famous woodcut and pristine dark of 1744.
    Click the Han Dynasty silk atlas of 'pheasants', Babylonian tablets,
    click Augustus Caesar's denarius, the 'hairy star' stitched at Bayeux,
    click Giotto's *Adoration,* Halley's sooty core (fluffy fractal aggregates)

– all answer Frequently Asked Questions. McNaught fades
    among the Southern Lights of a geomagnetic storm.
    A circumpolar object through Indus and Tucana.
    Probably tens of thousands, if ever it returns.

Saqqara

Horus sees, sees with sun and moon,
his left eye waxing and waning
as falcons are dipped in tar or salted in natron.

Wrapped in linen, bird-masked
and sold in oblong earthen jars,
thousands stack the catacombs;

galleries of potted hawks
in a necropolis of bulls, baboons, ibis
and the swathed mud of faked votives.

Horus sees, sees with sun and moon,
the day eyed with jasper
when a man's heart weighs against the feather:

his arms those of the divine falcon,
his hair strewn,
nostrils inlaid by the wind,

eyebrows two serpents entwined,
lashes firm, coloured with sky,
and his lids, the bringers of peace.

Saqqara: site of an ancient Egyptian animal necropolis.
Horus: falcon-headed Egyptian god of the sky.

Dikra Ridha

You Are Still Alive

'Away, I'd rather sail away like a swan that's here and gone'
from the song: 'El Condor Pasa' (If I could)

'Away, I'd rather sail away like a swan
that's here and gone.' But you can't
father, because the life you left in the snow

still lives on. I burrow your memories
because your pain can live in my veins.
I inherit your longing and the regrets

you left behind. Your footprints melted
when the season began to end. It ended
when you accepted fate without asking

questions. Questions that may have saved
your mind from lugging the weight
of time as you aged. It sounds muffled

on the songs your friends recorded
for you. The words you danced to are old
but not to me, father. I am your heir.

I carry your laughter in the memory
I was born with. And over your friends'
graves, seeds of longing grow

for the bees to pollinate new seedlings
and streams of melted snow
will swim in seas that rise to flood

the land. Butterflies will carry golden
moments to every garden and flower.
Like your daughter, your old laughter

blossoms and honey sweetens the seasons
of your dances. *'Away, I'd rather sail away
like a swan that's here and gone'* you say

but your songs will be heard in the sunshine
of every sky; above snow, in your country
and beyond the clouds. Your laughter

will live no matter how you forget your fate.
*Like a man who gets tied up to the ground
and gives the earth its saddest sound.* Father,

fate took you from country to country
hoping one day you'll return but here
I am, father, playing El Condor Pasa

for the grey clouds and willow trees
as they look into rivers of the mind.
Even if you live without remembering,

the bees will make sweet honey
with your old smile. Your footprints
in the snow will relive in every season

so gardens and flowers sing your songs
despite your need to forget forgetting.
'But away, I'd rather sail away like a swan

that's here and gone' – and every decade
father, I learn more about sacrifice and love.
Why we say yes to fate and its warnings.

A fate can kill you before your body. It leaves
you wandering this earth, tossing and turning,
refrying your decisions, watching your regrets

flourish in your children and a man gets tied
up to the ground, father. *He gives the earth
its saddest sound* – its saddest sound.

The Right to Be Wrong

The mixture had been perfecting
for decades, yet people

live their days as if nothing
could happen. What could happen

when the desire for oil is so strong?
Human beings would let it go – it only

belongs to earth but the chemical
mixture had an ultimate goal: the loudest

blast, the largest crater in the street.
Where are Samer's dreams, his dives

in the Tigris, the dog he chased, the apples
he crunched, the bread dough held in little

hands and delivered to mum at dawn
All that parenting and college debates,

his story and the decades of making
a mark on his land. Where are Muna's

memories, her tears over a boy and giggles
with little friends, the Yes's and No's

and all her daydreams at the desk?
The admin papers were checked,

signed, sent and received. Promises
exchanged. Those men and women

who God gave life – how wrong
is it to blow them like seventies' dolls?

How wrong is it to be right when a river
cries, a people die and a culture dries –

to break human beings and scatter
them on the street, to turn ancestors

to waste. Those cheeks that blushed
when kissed, the eyes that cried for mum

have died unclosed – the bombs
were made by men and women

who wake to sunshine, larks' song
and milkweed at the windowsill.

Their human rights are apples on a tree,
a law protects every apple and leaf.

They pat their cats, focus on happiness
and sip green tea perusing pictures

of beautifully formed bomb shells
they so carefully scaled, made, filled

and sealed. Was money worth their time?
What crossed their minds when they fired

the missiles? And without reply
the question rises like a siren:

how do men and women devise
for other men and women to die?

Marianne Burton

Scribblings on the Storehouse Wall

They could belong to Pompeii, most of these,
in sentiment and indelicacy,

displaying a brevity worthy of headline,
admirable to anyone

with a sensitivity to ephemera. Here sex
and excrement are mixed

with other desires too secret to be expressed
except on gypsum where

box-handlers and forklift operatives pass.
Each phrase foams rabid.

Each stroke of the calligrapher's brush
manifests satisfaction

that finally these matters have been spat
away leaving the spitter

clean after his frenzy of penmanship,
freed from his fardel,

like Midas's barber who whispered
down a field's rent

in spring never minding the wheat
might rustle it at harvest

ass's ears ass's ears
ass's ears

Moscow: Snow: Women in Furs

How odd they look these women in furs
when we can wear no furs in England.

The snow like little bits of lint brushes past
their faces and the stoles round their shoulders

and they smile as it tickles and flirts
as if contrast of warmth against freeze

is funny when you only taste it on tongues
and on made-up eyes caught in the street

between warmth of blue leather and warmth
of white marble. They laugh because mascara

hates the wet before they strut for the steps.
Their hair is naked to the air for seconds

between car suspension and restaurant velvet,
between walnut dash and red mahogany.

What fragile creatures, borrowing warmth
when one might think they have so much to spare.

So strokable. Each filament separate
and glossy as well-reduced jus of lamb.

My final stare catches pelts being draped,
dropped, thrown across a concierge's liveried arms,

while their own arms link like golden chains,
bare and golden in the hot breath of the night.

Steve Spence

Adapting to the Situation

Are ideas important
in art? What's being
talked about here is
gender-equality yet there
is no chance of an
immediate coup and
we're in for a severe
pruning. Here we have
a massive squandering
of talent. 'Yes, but it's
the repetition of these
images which creates
a sense of boredom',
he said. What is it that
you want me to do?
'Such wonky variation',
she said. Yet we scoured
the streets for junk and
for the throwaway textures
of the city. Who knows
what may lurk beneath
the turbulent current?
Your hours may not be
specified but payment
will be made on submission
of a monthly pay claim.
Are you a wild-eyed loon
standing at the gates of
oblivion? 'First of all,
it's wrong to blame the
zander', he said. Are you

suppressing your painterly
touch? Meanwhile, some-
thing big has grabbed hold
at last and it's time to start
talking in riddles again.

A Vehicle Approaches

Whoever it is
they are living
on borrowed
time. Are we
talking process
or product here?
Delicate fabrics
may be another
matter but some-
times an iceberg
will flip right
over in front of
your eyes. In this
instance it's not
so clear cut though
for some reason
you haven't taken
this into consideration.
Of course, the secret
of parsley soup
lies in the parsley
yet this issue is one
of consumption,
not production.
'That old moon
river', she said,

'it's wider than
a mile'. Do you
see a connection
between loneliness
and inner voices?
A message in a
bottle which has
washed up more
than 100 years
after it was thrown
in the sea has been
confirmed as the
world's oldest.

Reading the Water

Once again we're
looking at a soft
target. 'You don't
go skinny-dipping
with snapping turtles',
he said. Yet it could
be that plagiarism
is a key intellectual
device and young,
rigorous shoots are
what we want. Should
we welcome the era
of driverless cars?
Here's the dent, made
by the heel as it hits
the ground running.
How real are the tensions
at the top of the party?

'No, it's not a different thing entirely', he said. For those in thrall to its ideas representation is dead yet this swim has all the hallmarks of a hotspot. 'It's a projection, not a fact', he said, 'and our aim is always to build legitimacy'. It's a big, open expanse of water and there are few trees. Today there will be fireworks.

Jennifer Spector

The Arrow

> *Take the diamonds from your hair and lay them down.*
> *The deer-grass is thin. The timothy is brown.*
> *The shadow of an external world comes near.*
> —Wallace Stevens

   Now   the winds
sail disquiet
      scour the fields
           for that heart in port

      who is sounding at the breaks
         slippering dark rooms
   what shards and glyphs chisel
       camber in the heart?

where I have landed
     there is bark to be carried
          and plinths to root

      blistered with scorch
         the ghetto flower

         it is the hour   we who have wildered
     burn our cressets
      turn back to the road
   outskirt the village
try our broken drums

something
>	luffed in the wind
>	>	caught like bloom &

>	must on the whaled skiff
>	where I am laid

ferries me

>	say the dryland arrows
>	also are turning

Autumn

                  unfurls her
           orange leaves
        her gray morning
     with the birds
        threshing redding hulls

& that premonition
        we call winter

revisits every tree

*

                       however brief
                                return
changed by the route took

Sarah James

Penelope's Dream of Global Warming

The sky is a red shroud raining
flakes of dead star. Ithaca
has swum off, Greece's shoreline
retreated, leaving scattered islands.
Her husband's ship is a bestiary
with unmuzzled petrol breath.
The horned helm rocks, unsteady.

Her troubled sleep shivers and twists
with each wave that tips his sea.

Beached on an electric eel,
naked men crawl on all fours
along taut ropes that battle the wind.
Hooks yanked from green-field scales
leave brown gashes that bleed methane.
Flames crackle a cauldron;
its oil-black magic bubbled dry.

Baby fish rush to drown
in their mother's choked jaw.

A needle glints in Penelope's fingers,
as she watches her great-great-great-
grandchildren pierce their own skin
with piece after piece of sharp metal,
until they glisten with sweat and blood.
Beads of smoke and shredded light
thread their wet tapestry.

When she stretches her dream
to unstitch it, the yarn pulls tight.

3 a.m.

The night is clear and sharp –
as it can only be once lights sleep,
traffic dies and there's no one else
to see it, yet no happy genius or 'danse russe'
in my stepping, wild-haired
and pyjama-clad, into its peaty cleanness;
the almost-full moon boldly states
this is not a poem, this
is one long, deep breath.

Inhaling as told, I swallow the night
like a crisp communion wafer
floating on a cold ocean.
The moon that swells my throat
is a spring onion's layered bulb,
uncrunched by teeth. A lone star
tickles. The rest slides down
with the slight burn of malt whisky,
then a slow, slow peace.

Nathan Shepherdson

a ladder cannot be convinced to climb down from itself

. i watch him knit a mirror with his eyes

watch him cast the first stone into original memory
to see it skim towards the same mirror
now propped up against the horizon
shattered like glass fingernails from a wailing wall
as we ourselves alternate as gold teeth
exploding inside this mica mouth
spines smelted into the slightest answers
inside our own ears floating in open ocean
as wishing wells for the drowned
as deep as any word our heads pop up
to compete for the dot on the i in genesis

your licence to create the opening dream sequence has been revoked

enclosed are the instructions
on how to design a life
while walking the dog
so it can sniff out the bones
in your own grave

)…strike gently away from body…(

in a downbeat of the psyche
your necklace lets go
scattering toes & fingers
in Bren gun slow audio
across the heirloom oak table

in another Pacific War drama
shot through a Vaseline lens

)…strike gently away from body…(

you stop in at the dry cleaner
to collect your skin only to be told
that the stains cannot be removed
without extra cost and that the only currency
accepted in this establishment is the soul

)…strike gently away from body…(

this list is predetermined:

> 1 stand here while your tongue is dissolved in water
> 2 spend more time teaching dust to speak
> 3 permit yourself to learn the botanical names of lies

without regret i fall into my father's mouth
sucked back through his cigar butt
spat onto his bullock's eye

asleep his eyelids become trampolines
rebounding one eternal seed
between here & hereafter
blindsided he sees everything in his wake

the soft grenade in his hand contains no messages for the future

i watch him separate each lip of its colour
before these words form

)…strike gently away from body…(

orbiting shadows
intervene with grace
in a burning wheelchair

to let down what we couldn't lift
to let down what we couldn't lift

you catch yourself wading
through your own ability
to scold the light

you take aim at the world
with one thought & realise you are
the target ←

you catch yourself wading
through your own ability
to scold the light for being silent

)…strike gently away from body…(

how to replace the washer
to stop blood leeching into the cloud
above your head

do you remember
how we would hover
above each other in sleep

how we perfected the art
of waking up in the wrong body
at the right time

in our blinking our jellyfish propulsion through evolution

i was the first person in history to close a door .

Colin Campbell Robinson

from the kafka variations

Beyond a certain point there is no return. This point has to be reached.
Franz Kafka

4.
Sometimes he leaves home suddenly and, half prepared, walks to his office and wonders why is he there on Sunday.

Noise, peace, the typewriter and birdsong: trains rattling along the track; the organ grinder.

The case was already lost in any case.

5.
Devout.

Delicate.

Intense.

Vision.

Underground fire.

Unspeakable.

    Some of his words.

Fragment (consider revising)

6.
Is it our fault the day ends before it begins? One moment sees dawn, the next, creeping dusk.

And what of yesterday already distant and tomorrow about to rise?

November the sixth: the path covered with dry leaves, once more.

7.
Do you receive visitors? Are they scholars speaking in an unknown tongue, as unknown as you are in their land, as unknown as you are to your neighbours?

8.
All those villa experiences: those days on the Algarve; in Antibes; winding through Bordeaux mouthing the vintage; all those days before the fall.

Impatience.
Indolence.
Or impatience.

Either way heaven is in our mind or is hanging by a thread.

9.
Found, a letter from Schopenhauer:

Becoming old, drawing together, everything has died away around us.

We are living more and more in the memories of the past.

Sensible deliberation and a firm will are not enough, there is an instinctive impulse, like a demoniacal urge, that guides, careless of everything else.

Thus we may live to see something in the end, if we know how to live to be very old.

10.
—Who has lost the right track forever?
—To what indifference may people come?
—Who has a 'profound conviction'?

And in his rooms he entertains her thus, after she'd climbed the stairs, the stairs moving ever upward like tireless waves.

11.
The wrong door, a lone stranger at table (oil lamp and staff), time passing slow: close the door quietly, forget your mistake.

12
He hangs the toys in his linen press in case someone comes to play. But no one does and the letters he sends are unanswered.

13.
Even though they know things must change, nothing changes. This is because they change nothing, for fear of change.

Did the cage find the bird?

14.
And the misery brewed by a city pervades the air when the southerly is still.

He wants somewhere to live but is always outbid.

Who has misty prospects while wearing heavy boots?

He describes overcrowding with such precision.

Everyone is grey.

15.
For a moment he dwells in the tropics constructing a railway, but it is only for a moment.

The mosquitoes buzz dissatisfied.

From a real angler no fish escapes. Discuss, citing your own experience.

16.
The lucky cat led the way in those days; today the fox leads down icy roads lined by the guardians of misfortune.

What choice do you have when it comes to your Father's legacy? What choice do you have when the city calls?

At the gates, he waits.

17.
Is the past so obscure it has hidden an eighth wonder or even a ninth?

History is the history of false beginnings.

Maybe Brod obeyed.

Dennis Barone

Recipe

Norwegians are by nature quiet; often tall and blond haired.
I am none of these things and yet I am Norwegian, a fact few know.
My mother's parents left Norway for Rose Hill, Virginia and then
moved west to Fort Dodge, Iowa and west again to San Francisco
where they opened the Cow Palace Diner. Today I meet a friend
every Friday morning for breakfast. We have a list of six or seven
          places,
all of them in central Connecticut. He orders omelets. I order pancakes
or French toast; sometimes eggs over easy. And I never say
I'm Norwegian: on that I'm silent.

A First Book

On the boat a dear familiar face stopped between stone steps
and a clump of rushes. On the other side of the river, moonlight
and starlight. A beautiful voice interrupted by laughter and
thenceforward all letters for many years would go to the desert.
The sight of their dog did not make our world an open door.
Wonderful things could not take them both, or the woods, oil
paneling, doves, burning oil, clothes, the window, her hat.
This setting, this sternness: each had only these things to
remember and could comment for a minute that the scene
would soon close. I might have known the essential truth:

past, present, idyll, present.

Baedeker

To the north, a bare hill
The sky a mixture of music, food
Vast forests – the beauty not revealing
It was there in every corner

And it will continue in our room
Something good about the paint; our chance, bright
Only in part correct and followed by
Their dark eyes, skin the color of bronze

This is what you do then
Serve up the double portion as we gather
This is what you do then
Three levels of high end luxury, the possible

The house was near, dwarfed by distance
Bound up passions, feuds, the palm
Here lay the meaning, they stayed away
Flies swarmed at the table

Here and there was a house drawing light
White in the sun the walls of bare clay
Narrow barred windows fierce and embarrassed
Other quarters as if bow legs and blank eyes

Gave an effect shapeless and wrinkled
Out of bounds, impersonal, little breathing-space
Everyone knows the hostile workings of the expense
Half-sunk in the ground and continued

Once upon a time the houses were all alike
Every now and then the doors of some
Never failed to hold the same thing
The paper shiny with a promise

Even to speak to their hearts
Is something constantly never (set)
How to talk what is opposed to stars
The great news never came back

Huddled together with shirt-sleeves rolled
Gray weather and windy, a gentle drizzle
All the players looked out the window
The cards that evening fell

Rough weather turning cold at night
The house in a shapeless ocean
And a wind released from across
The clearing embittered and poor

Snow perhaps the eclipse swung
Between these shadows these precise terms
No appeal for an old palette shapeless
Masses of color elusive, mysterious

In the house a face appeared at the window
This is what you do then
This is what you do then

Elżbieta Wójcik-Leese

wabi sabi for beginners

it's when you take off your sunglasses to have a closer look through the binoculars at that lighthouse on the curve of the promontory. but instead of slipping the glasses into your bag, you prop them on your head, even though you're wearing a thick woollen hat and you think, these frames will not like it. now northwesterly chill makes you reach for the hood, and as you're pulling it up, the glasses, knocked off, land on the stones of Rosmarkie Beach

and no licking or swearing can restore them

it's when your elderly father goes to hospital for screening tests, because you've finally convinced your mother that nurses there will make sure he drinks all the necessary solutions, but still he succeeds in pouring out that drink. so the tests are rescheduled, pneumonia sets in and at 6:25 the doctor phones to say he's sorry

and no licking can restore

hereditary condition

I prop my naked leg on the edge of the bath tub and spread the moisturizer down my calf, observing the thick blue vein just below my knee, raised.

I regret that, thirty years back, I didn't come soon enough, when your shapely calves – women envied you! – were incised, your varicose veins tied shut and removed. I didn't realize you wanted me in the ward two days earlier. Not until I saw your thinner, almost sheepish, face: the blue of your eyes, usually strong, uncomfortably watered down. You were watching me imploringly, but also with rebuke.

Your twisted and bulging cords were now straight blue pyjama stripes, over the livid slits, and you felt threatened. Almost emasculated.

We're still in that hospital corridor: a twenty-something woman in high heels, shifting her weight awkwardly, from one leg to another, and a middle-aged man whose leg veins can hardly cope with the toughest job of carrying blood back to the heart, against gravity and restraint. Under so much pressure, the valves succumb.

Masayo Gôshi

translated by the author

Rental Locker Shop in Shinjuku

A rental locker shop opening around the clock
In Shinjuku
Where day-labourers keep their things
They come and unlock their own
To meet their belongings
It's a time of daydream
Their impassioned faces start radiating

A man with no job, no home
Rummaging through his shabby clothes and daily goods in his locker
Takes out a sheet of tattered paper
Invalid certificate of unemployment insurance
Which was issued by a company he worked for decades ago
    This is the only time I was treated as a human being
    This is the only document certifying who I was
He pats the paper by his hand as if it is a ritual
And puts it back in the locker
Seeming embarrassed to have mentioned something irrelevant
He resumes his earlier indifference
And goes out

A man who comes next
Takes a sack made from *furoshiki* out of his locker
And unfolds it
Inside, a set of carpenter's tools
Kept since the booming economy went bust
    They are not as sharp as they used to be
    But I can't throw them away
    I just want to use them once more,
    Brush up my carpentering skills
    Which I owe so much to my master

    Just once more before I die
    That's all
A smile appears on face for a moment
He bows courteously
And goes out

Another one to come
No family, no relatives, no job and no place to live
No right to live which the Constitution stipulates
No social security
Except Workmen's accident compensation insurance
Which is entitled to a lucky day-labourer too
    They say this is for workers
    But I know this is also to protect companies
    The law is versatile, you know
    The strong are more cunning, and get more than the weaker
    This is the reality
    You have to take care of yourself
    You have to take responsibility for yourself
    I have done many dangerous jobs
    Including at nuclear plants
    Many of my co-workers have died
    Without any compensation
    I've been all right so far
    But I shall die in a ditch
He shows his medical card recording the radiation level he has been
                                                                exposed to
He knows it's useless
Putting it back in his locker, he goes out
Raising his hand over his shoulder
See you then

The last person on the night
He looks like a smart salaried man
    What do you think I do?
    I collect rental cars all through the night
    It was hard at first but now I love it
His locker is full of CDs

Listening to music is my only pastime, be says
The Last Six Piano Sonatas by Beethoven,
I think it's his greatest musical challenge
Symphony No 1 by Brahms,
Seems a sign of his fear and anxiety, so conscious of Beethoven's
                                                                    Ninth
Likewise, Bruckner's No 9 and Mahler's No 9
And Schubert's *Impromptus* and Schumann's *Carnival*...
They are moving, expressive, and agony-filled
I'm in ecstasy
My tearful eyes are floating
On the road illuminated by headlights
A Milky Way
I have no religion but I know all about awe
This is the moment disconnected from society full of greed and
                                                                    malice
He puts the selected CDs into a bag
Among them was Richter's Schubert

Stars appear in the sky of Shinjuku

Angry Cabbages
Overgrown cabbages waiting to be harvested burst out crying

From a beam in the barn one evening
A father's body
Hangs heavily
It triggered a succession of creaking sounds
From cabbages in the backyard

In the morning
The father went around the cabbage field
Rubbing the head of each forbidden cabbage
The night before, in a meeting
He'd even talked about the future with his colleagues
And showed his positive outlook in words
Nobody expected his death

The cabbages' outcry can be heard
Being forced to curb their vibrant growth
Must be cruel
Their anger, poking through their full-fledged leaves,
Becomes a cracking sound
It is a deep mourning for the father

Fuhyo : (damage due to groundless rumours of contamination)
Such a convenient word
To conceal unforeseeable damage!
The son listened to the mourning of the cabbages
Without moving
Trying not to miss the slightest sound

When the disturbing sound ceased
Anger and sorrow swelled up in his heart all at once
And blew up
And his angry cabbages left inside
Began falling apart one by one
Heartbroken

Szymon Słomczyński

translated by Elżbieta Wójcik-Leese

Sharpening

claws against vantage points you need to adopt?
Not at all. For a mutual exchange adopt
exclusively crime plots. Those with a motive
and the covering of tracks. Time: way back. Place:
young Orthodox church, the paint still fresh. Victim:
a man in his thirties. From his shot-through side
spills pus, this crude spill cheapens at a fast rate
towards the foot. The rates don't rise, the feet pale down.

People are gathering, swarming – a grim throng.
Carrying candles. Above them, hands. Each shelters a flame,
none turns to a fist. In the swarm stand fathers
and sons. The sacrificed victim is their ghost.

It's a day before the anniversary of his birth. Tomorrow
he would have been born again if he could do it twice,
but even the simplest people don't believe he can.

It dawns. The priest speaks in a heinous voice:
Find his body and eat it – you will come to being.

And in the name of the holy trinity
do not leave this vantage point,
do not seek the killer behind this fatality.

Menno Wigman
translated by Judith Wilkinson

Life Story

I was ashamed of nearly everything.
My neck, my hair, my handwriting, my name,

the nerdy school bag that my mother gave me,
my father as he fumbled with his blazer,

the family home whose friendship I turned down.
But there are tubes now in my father's arm

and he speaks more and more hoarsely of goodbye.
My shame's crouched in a corner now. He died

the way he drove his Opel: in control,
correctly, eyes fixed firmly on the road.

He saw no point in a dumb fight with death.
How everything I still wanted to tell him

scattered under the wheels of time.

Pitying the Reader

A book? From cover to cover? I lack the strength.
Even poetry – just thinking about it –
exhausts me. I've overdosed on poems,
stare blindly at the pages of my books.
For many months I've had reader's block:

I've grown allergic to the alphabet.

And this poem that refuses to be a poem,
flat on its back and dying for some light,
for god's sake, what do I want with it?
Admit it to yourself, your lines won't run,
your mind a thing too delicate for words,

and you pitied the reader in the end.

Tuesday. A city eyeing itself. Not doing a thing,
nor wanting to. Death of a boyhood dream.
Ambition. Desire. All burnt out, done in.
Something to do with hubris, meagre fame
and a divine trauma I refuse to name.

Metropolitan

What she did pre-me? With Hugo she ate lobster,
with Thomas she drove through LA, with Sander
she slept in Berlin, with Jean, with Stein … and I,

so green about the secret algebra
of our pleasure: whose locks, whose lips, whose
glance do I see mirrored in her face?

She doesn't know her laugh is just like Lisa's.
And I don't see how Hugo is like me.
But six weeks on, an audience of ghosts

has gathered in a circle round our bed,
to watch our slow, sweet, desperate attempts
to banish their deepest names from our heads.

Earth, Be Gentle

Earth, a virtuous body enters now.
In it a majestic sun once rose.
A summer month inhabited the eyes,
the midriff filled with mellow evening light
and round the heart a delicate moon stood guard.

The palms of the hands felt water, stroked pets,
the soles of the feet kissed sand, kissed stone. Insight.
A strange insight crept into the head, the tongue
grew sharp, fists hid inside the fingers,
the hands fought for bread, money, love and light.

You can read plenty of books on the subject.
You might write one yourself. Earth, be gentle
with this man who held a hundred keys or more
and now enters the dark without a compass
to spend his first night here.

Author's note: written/or the 144th municipal funeral in Amsterdam for a person with no family.

Notes on Contributors

DENNIS BARONE's latest book is *Beyond Memory: Italian Protestants in Italy and America* (SUNY Press, New York).

JAMES BELL lives in Brittany. He has two collections from Tall-Lighthouse, *the just vanished place* and *fishing for beginners*. His work also appears in the eBook, *A Compendium of Beasts* from Poetry Kit 2016 as a free download at http://www.poetrykit.org/Bestiary.pdf

MARIANNE BURTON's first collection, *She Inserts the Key* (Seren), was shortlisted for the Forward Prizes' Felix Dennis Award in 2013.

MAKYLA CURTIS is currently studying for an MA at the University of Auckland. Her work has previously appeared in a number of New Zealand publications (*IKA, Brief,* Blackmail press, *REM Magazine*).

MARK DICKINSON's first collection *Tender Geometries* was published by Shearsman in 2015. His work also featured in the anthology *The Ground Aslant* (Shearsman Books, 2011). He lives in Orkney.

MASAYO GÔSHI studied Art History at Keio University, Tokyo, and at Essex University, and English at Exeter University. She has published three collections of poetry in Japan, and has also translated the complete poems of Stevie Smith into Japanese. The poems here were written following a visit to the coastal location of the Fukushima nuclear accident.

KHALED HAKIM had work in the anthology, *foil: defining poetry 1985-2000* (etruscan books, 2000), but stopped writing for a number of years. This is an unpublished piece from before he stopped, and signals his return to poetry.

CAROLINE HAWKRIDGE has an MA in Creative Writing from Manchester Metropolitan University, and was poet-in-residence last year at the NHS National Aspergillosis Centre. She also runs the Hawkridge Agency, a literary management and promotion company.

JULIE IRIGARAY has been shortlisted for the *London Magazine* Poetry Prize (2016) and has had work in *Southword, Envoi* and *Tears in the Fence*. She is currently training as a literary translator in Dublin.

SARAH JAMES's most recent publications are *The Magnetic Diaries* (Knives, Forks and Spoons Press, 2015), *Plenty-Fish* (Nine Arches Press, 2015) and *Lampshades & Glass Rivers* (Lamplight Press, Loughborough, 2016).

PETER LARKIN has three books with Shearsman, and a fourth, *Introgression Latewood*, due for publication in late 2017.

JOHN LEVY is a retired attorney and public defender living in Tucson, Arizona, and was a contributing editor to the very first series of this magazine in 1981-1982. His books include *Oblivion, Tyrants, Crumbs* (Tel-Let,

2003), *Scribble & Expanse* (Tel-Let, 1995), *We Don't Kill Snakes Where We Come From* (Querencia Press, 1994). A recent e-book, *In the Pit of the Empty*, is available on the Otata blog and includes one of the poems here: https://otatablog.files.wordpress.com/2016/12/levy-in-the-pit-of-the-empty2.pdf

ROSANNA LICARI is an Australian writer, whose work has appeared in various journals and anthologies. Her poetry collection *An Absence of Saints* won the Thomas Shapcott Poetry Award, the Anne Elder Poetry Prize and the Wesley Michel Wright Prize for Poetry. She won the inaugural 2015 Philip Bacon Ekphrasis Poetry Prize for her poem 'The Wait'. Her website is www.rosanna.licari.com

ANN MATTHEWS is an avant-garde musician with 14 LPs to her name, and is a writer of poetry and short fiction. She has had two collections from Knives Forks and Spoons Press, *Strangeways* (2014) and *Losing Boundaries* (2016). She has spent most of her life in North Wales and moved to the Northeast 4 years ago to complete a Ph.D in Creative Writing at Northumbria University. She is currently working as a gardener and walking on, and writing about, the North Pennine fells.

DAVID MILLER's Collected Poems, *Reassembling Still*, was published by Shearsman Books in 2014. He has recently co-edited the *Selected Poems* of Alfred Celestine, *Weightless Word*, also for Shearsman Books.

KATE MILLER lives in London and her first full collection, *The Observances*, was published by Carcanet/Oxford Poets. This was shortlisted for the 2015 Costa Award, and won the Seamus Heaney Centre First Collection Prize. In 2012 she completed her Ph.D while teaching courses in poetry in the English Department at Goldsmiths, University of London.

MICHELLE PENN grew up in the US, lived in France for many years, and is a naturalised British citizen. Her poetry has appeared in *The Wolf*, as well as in several issues of *Runes*, *Spillway* and other US literary magazines. She is currently working on two poetry collections and a novel.

FRANCES PRESLEY is the author of three volumes from Shearsman, most recently *Halse for hazel* (2014). Her translations of the Norwegian poet Hanne Bramness are also published by Shearsman, with a further such collection due later in 2017.

DIKRA RIDHA was selected in 2014 as a Next Generation Poet by the Poetry Book Society, and is an Iraqi British Poet and translator. Her first pamphlet, *There Are No Americans in Baghdad's Bird Market,* was published in 2009.

COLIN CAMPBELL ROBINSON is an Australian writer and photographer currently living in Rothesay. Recently his work has appeared in *Otoliths*, *BlazeVox*, *Molly Bloom* and *e-ratio* among others. Knives Forks and Spoons published his collection *Blue Solitude – a self-portrait in six scenarios* this year.

PETER ROBINSON has a number of books published by Shearsman, most recently – and most importantly – his *Collected Poems 1975-2016* (2017).

JULIE SAMPSON's collection, *Tessitura* (2013) and her edition of Mary, Lady Chudleigh's *Selected Poems* (2009) were published by Shearsman Books.

ALEXANDRA SASHE is Russian, lives in Vienna and writes in English. She has one collection from Shearsman (*Antibodies*, 2013), and a second, *Convalescence Dance*, due in late 2017.

NATHAN SHEPHERDSON lives in Queensland and is the author of is five books of poetry. He has won a number of major prizes including the Thomas Shapcott Award and Josephine Ulrick Prize. His most recent collection is *the day the artists stood still (vol 1.)* (Another Lost Shark, Brisbane, 2013).

SZYMON SŁOMCZYŃSKI (b. 1988) has published two poetry collections: *Nadjeżdża* (It's Coming, 2013; shortlisted for the NIKE Prize, the most prestigious literary prize in Poland; winner of the prize for best first collection, 2013) and *Dwupłat* (Biplane, 2015). His poetry has not previously appeared in English.

JENNIFER SPECTOR is a poet from New York City, living and working in Panama. Her poetry has appeared or is forthcoming in *Fulcrum: an annual of poetry and aesthetics, Reliquiae: A Journal of Contemporary and Historical Responses to Landscape & Nature, La Vague, Molly Bloom* and in *Suelo* vol. 1. Her website can be found at http://www.jenniferspectorstudio.com

STEVE SPENCE has two collections from Shearsman Books, most recently *Maelstrom Origami* (2015). He lives in Plymouth.

MENNO WIGMAN (b. 1966) is regarded as one of the finest poets of his generation in the Netherlands. He has published five full-length collections to date, the most recent being *Slordig met Geluk* (Squandering happiness). Wigman is also an editor, essayist and a prolific translator. In 2012-2013 he was the city poet of Amsterdam.

Wigman regularly takes part in a scheme organised by the municipality of Amsterdam whereby poets are invited to write a poem for the funeral of a person who has no family or friends to mourn them (homeless or elderly people). 'Earth, Be Gentle', included in this selection, was such a poem.

JUDITH WILKINSON grew up in the Netherlands and is fully bilingual, but only translates into English. She has won many awards, including the Popescu Prize for European Poetry in Translation in 2011 and the Brockway Prize in 2013. In 2011 her work as a whole was nominated for a London Poetry Award. She lives in Groningen.

ELŻBIETA WÓJCIK-LEESE writes with/in English, Polish and Danish. Her poems have appeared in *Other Countries: Contemporary Poets Rewiring History* (2014), *Metropoetica (Poetry and urban space: Women writing cities)* (Seren, 2013) and in *Long Poem Magazine* and *Modern Poetry in Translation. Nothing More* (Arc, 2013) which samples the Polish poet Krystyna Miłobędzka, was shortlisted for the 2015 Popescu European Poetry Translation Prize.

www.ingramcontent.com/pod-product-compliance
Lightning Source LLC
Chambersburg PA
CBHW030957090426
42737CB00007B/580